YOU KNOW YOU'RE A REPUBLICAN DEMOCRAT if...

— FRANK BENJAMIN —

SOURCEBOOKS HYSTERIA™
AN IMPRINT OF SOURCEBOOKS, INC.®
NAPERVILLE, ILLINOIS

Published by Sourcebooks, Inc.
P.O. Box 4410, Naperville, Illinois 60567-4410
(630) 961-3900
FAX: (630) 961-2168
www.sourcebooks.com

Library of Congress Cataloging-in-Publication Data

Benjamin, Frank.
  You know you're a Republican/Democrat if... / by Frank Benjamin.
    p. cm.
  ISBN 1-4022-0333-0 (alk. paper)
  1. Republican Party (U.S.)—Humor. 2. Democratic Party (U.S.)—
Humor. I. Title.

 PN6231.P6B39 2004
 818'.602—dc22

                                    2004012510

               Printed and bound in Canada
         WC 10 9 8 7 6 5 4 3 2 1

"Politics is the best show in America. I love animals and I love politicians and I love to watch both of them back home in their native states or after they have been captured and sent to the zoo or to Washington."

—Will Rogers, 1894

YOU KNOW YOU'RE A
REPUBLICAN if...

★ ★ ★

You start off on third base and think you've hit a triple.

YOU KNOW YOU'RE A
DEMOCRAT if...

★ ★ ★

You hit a single but believe
you deserve a triple because
the other team got one.

YOU KNOW YOU'RE A
REPUBLICAN if...

★ ★ ★

You believe the U.S. Constitution
clearly supports strip mining.

YOU KNOW YOU'RE A
DEMOCRAT if...

★ ★ ★

You believe the U.S. Constitution
clearly supports strippers.

YOU KNOW YOU'RE A
REPUBLICAN if...

★ ★ ★

You think Colin Powell might
make a good president if
he weren't black.

YOU KNOW YOU'RE A
DEMOCRAT if...

★ ★ ★

You think Colin Powell might
make a good president if
he weren't conservative.

YOU KNOW YOU'RE A
REPUBLICAN if...

★ ★ ★

You can't stand your gay uncle,
but you invite him to your
son's wedding because he's rich.

YOU KNOW YOU'RE A
DEMOCRAT if...

★ ★ ★

You can't stand your rich uncle, but you invite him to your daughter's graduation party because he's gay.

YOU KNOW YOU'RE A
REPUBLICAN if...

★ ★ ★

You can't fathom that Abraham Lincoln was actually a Republican!

YOU KNOW YOU'RE A
DEMOCRAT if...

★ ★ ★

You can't fathom that Abraham Lincoln was actually a Republican!

11

YOU KNOW YOU'RE A
REPUBLICAN if...

★ ★ ★

You wouldn't mind if the
Commonwealth of Massachusetts
seceded from the Union.

YOU KNOW YOU'RE A
DEMOCRAT if...

★ ★ ★

You wish the Republic of Texas had never become a state.

YOU KNOW YOU'RE A
REPUBLICAN if...

★ ★ ★

You think the only truly
honorable revolution in the
history of mankind was the
American Revolution.

YOU KNOW YOU'RE A
DEMOCRAT if...

★ ★ ★

You think the only good
revolution is the one you're
personally going to lead.

YOU KNOW YOU'RE A
REPUBLICAN if...

★ ★ ★

You have a tender spot in your heart for corporate tax attorneys.

YOU KNOW YOU'RE A
DEMOCRAT if...

★ ★ ★

You have a tender spot in
your heart for product liability
trial lawyers.

YOU KNOW YOU'RE A
REPUBLICAN if...

★ ★ ★

You're planning to name your
firstborn son "Dubya."

YOU KNOW YOU'RE A
DEMOCRAT if...

★ ★ ★

You're planning to name your firstborn son "Hillary."

YOU KNOW YOU'RE A
REPUBLICAN if...

★ ★ ★

You favor free speech, except for
burning the flag or criticizing
U.S. military policy.

YOU KNOW YOU'RE A
DEMOCRAT if...

★ ★ ★

You favor free speech, except for ugly words about minorities, the disabled, or endangered species.

YOU KNOW YOU'RE A
REPUBLICAN if...

★ ★ ★

You own plaid pants.

YOU KNOW YOU'RE A
DEMOCRAT if...

★ ★ ★

You own a plaid bowtie.

YOU KNOW YOU'RE A
REPUBLICAN if...

★ ★ ★

You've watched the movie
The Dirty Dozen six times, and
every time you cried at the end.

YOU KNOW YOU'RE A
DEMOCRAT if...

★ ★ ★

You cried watching *Bambi* as
a kid, and you've been in
therapy ever since.

YOU KNOW YOU'RE A
REPUBLICAN if...

★ ★ ★

Your favorite pastimes are reading *Forbes*, relaxing at your beach condo, and cheating at golf.

YOU KNOW YOU'RE A
DEMOCRAT if...

★ ★ ★

Your favorite pastimes are reading the *New Republic*, visiting used bookstores, and cheating at golf.

YOU KNOW YOU'RE A
REPUBLICAN if...

★ ★ ★

You own a 30-foot ocean-going
speedboat named
Just Desserts.

YOU KNOW YOU'RE A
DEMOCRAT if...

★ ★ ★

You own a 30-foot sailboat named
Guilty Pleasure.

YOU KNOW YOU'RE A
REPUBLICAN if...

★ ★ ★

Your high school class voted you
"Most Likely to Wear Pinstripes
or Prison Stripes."

YOU KNOW YOU'RE A DEMOCRAT if...

★ ★ ★

Your high school class voted you
"Most Likely to Change Gender."

31

YOU KNOW YOU'RE A
REPUBLICAN if...

★ ★ ★

Your father's favorite saying was,
"Only the strong survive."

YOU KNOW YOU'RE A
DEMOCRAT if...

★ ★ ★

Your father's favorite saying was,
"Remember the Golden Rule."

YOU KNOW YOU'RE A
REPUBLICAN if...

★ ★ ★

You think John Kennedy "stole" the 1960 presidential election because of vote tampering by Chicago's Mayor Daley.

YOU KNOW YOU'RE A
DEMOCRAT if...

★ ★ ★

You think George W. Bush "stole" the 2000 presidential election because of vote tampering by the U.S. Supreme Court.

YOU KNOW YOU'RE A
REPUBLICAN if...

★ ★ ★

You prove your racial sensitivity by
saying *gracias* to your gardener.

YOU KNOW YOU'RE A
DEMOCRAT if...

★ ★ ★

You're strongly committed to
racial equality even if you don't
personally know anyone of a
different race.

YOU KNOW YOU'RE A
REPUBLICAN if...

★ ★ ★

You have a picture of yourself
shaking hands with Ronald Reagan
hanging on your office wall.

YOU KNOW YOU'RE A
DEMOCRAT if...

★ ★ ★

You have a picture of
Ronald Reagan hanging in the
middle of your dartboard.

YOU KNOW YOU'RE A
REPUBLICAN if...

★ ★ ★

Your favorite initials are
NRA, GWB, FOX, and WSJ.

YOU KNOW YOU'RE A
DEMOCRAT if...

★ ★ ★

Your favorite initials are
WPA, JFK, AFL-CIO, and MLK.

YOU KNOW YOU'RE A
REPUBLICAN if...

★ ★ ★

At some point in your life you
have won a skeet shooting trophy,
a steeplechase riding trophy,
or a trophy wife.

YOU KNOW YOU'RE A
DEMOCRAT if...

★ ★ ★

You received the
Good Conduct Award
in grade school.

YOU KNOW YOU'RE A
REPUBLICAN if...

★ ★ ★

Your excuse for buying
a gas-guzzling SUV is,
"Mind your own business!"

YOU KNOW YOU'RE A
DEMOCRAT if...

★ ★ ★

Your excuse for buying a gas-guzzling SUV is, "Umm, I plan to deliver Meals on Wheels in wilderness areas."

YOU KNOW YOU'RE A
REPUBLICAN if...

★ ★ ★

You have a good stock portfolio,
but your conscience is nagging you
about your big investment in
tobacco companies.

YOU KNOW YOU'RE A
DEMOCRAT if...

★ ★ ★

You have a good conscience,
but you really miss the days
when smoking was fun.

YOU KNOW YOU'RE A
REPUBLICAN if...

★ ★ ★

You've accepted the fact that
Oprah Winfrey is filthy rich
because she worked hard
for her money.

YOU KNOW YOU'RE A
DEMOCRAT if...

★ ★ ★

You're proud of how successful
Oprah Winfrey has become, as
long as she contributes big checks
to the right causes.

49

YOU KNOW YOU'RE A
REPUBLICAN if...

★ ★ ★

The bumper sticker on your
Jaguar says, "Money can't buy
love, but it can buy cars."

YOU KNOW YOU'RE A
DEMOCRAT if...

★ ★ ★

The bumper sticker
on your VW bug says,
"Make gas, don't burn it."

YOU KNOW YOU'RE A
REPUBLICAN if...

★ ★ ★

You believe it's a cryin' shame
not everyone gets stock options.

YOU KNOW YOU'RE A
DEMOCRAT if...

★ ★ ★

You believe the government
should give everyone free,
low-water-consumption toilets.

YOU KNOW YOU'RE A
REPUBLICAN if...

★ ★ ★

You give a beggar your business card, invite him to come apply for a job, and walk away feeling smug.

YOU KNOW YOU'RE A
DEMOCRAT if...

★ ★ ★

You give a beggar a dollar bill
and walk away worrying he
will spend it on booze.

YOU KNOW YOU'RE A
REPUBLICAN if...

★ ★ ★

You write to your congressman in defense of the interest income tax deduction for vacation homes.

YOU KNOW YOU'RE A
DEMOCRAT if...

★ ★ ★

You write to your congresswoman
and suggest a $1 tax return
checkoff for endangered jellyfish.

YOU KNOW YOU'RE A
REPUBLICAN if...

★ ★ ★

You want to increase the
U.S. military budget, especially
for the base in your
congressional district.

YOU KNOW YOU'RE A
DEMOCRAT if...

★ ★ ★

You want to slash the
U.S. military budget, as long as
they don't touch the base in your
congressional district.

YOU KNOW YOU'RE A
REPUBLICAN if...

★ ★ ★

You sent flowers and a thank you
card to Monica Lewinsky.

YOU KNOW YOU'RE A
DEMOCRAT if...

★ ★ ★

You can't imagine what
Clinton saw in Monica when
he has such a hottie for a wife.

YOU KNOW YOU'RE A
REPUBLICAN if...

★ ★ ★

You've thought about becoming a
Libertarian, but you have trouble
with their philosophical support of
prostitution, gay marriage, and
uninhibited personal freedom.

YOU KNOW YOU'RE A
DEMOCRAT if...

★ ★ ★

You've thought about becoming a
Libertarian, but you have trouble
with their support of free trade.

YOU KNOW YOU'RE A
REPUBLICAN if...

★ ★ ★

You're afraid of the IRS.

YOU KNOW YOU'RE A
DEMOCRAT if...

★ ★ ★

You're afraid of the FBI.

YOU KNOW YOU'RE A
REPUBLICAN if...

★ ★ ★

You buy a big gas-guzzling SUV, thus sending American dollars to Middle Eastern countries where everyone hates America.

YOU KNOW YOU'RE A
DEMOCRAT if...

★ ★ ★

You buy a modest Japanese,
German, or Swedish car,
thus sending American dollars
to European countries where
everyone hates America.

YOU KNOW YOU'RE A
REPUBLICAN if...

★ ★ ★

You don't think public buildings
need to be wheelchair accessible,
but you believe public lands
should be open to anyone with
an oil rig or an ATV.

YOU KNOW YOU'RE A
DEMOCRAT if...

★ ★ ★

You think every building, including the top of the Washington Monument, should be accessible to anyone using a wheelchair or Seeing Eye dog, but public lands should be wilderness areas open only to those who can hike five miles in and out.

YOU KNOW YOU'RE A
REPUBLICAN if...

★ ★ ★

You think public education is
broken and doesn't deserve more
money, and you send your children
to an expensive private school.

YOU KNOW YOU'RE A
DEMOCRAT if...

★ ★ ★

You think public education is the backbone of America, it just needs more money, and you send your children to an expensive private school.

YOU KNOW YOU'RE A
REPUBLICAN if...

★ ★ ★

You attend a "Save the Wilderness" charity dinner, and, while the speaker is rambling on, you daydream about which sauce would taste good on broiled spotted owl.

YOU KNOW YOU'RE A
DEMOCRAT if...

★ ★ ★

You refuse to attend the
"Save the Wilderness" charity
dinner because the chicken being
served isn't free range.

YOU KNOW YOU'RE A
REPUBLICAN if...

★ ★ ★

You think a president's spouse
should stand by her man through
thick and thin.

YOU KNOW YOU'RE A
DEMOCRAT if...

★ ★ ★

You think a president's spouse should stand behind her man until he's out of office and she can run for the office herself.

YOU KNOW YOU'RE A
REPUBLICAN if...

★ ★ ★

You think White House interns
should serve the president loyally.

YOU KNOW YOU'RE A
DEMOCRAT if...

★ ★ ★

You think White House interns
should service the president royally.

YOU KNOW YOU'RE A
REPUBLICAN if...

★ ★ ★

You think the movie
Conan the Barbarian is a great
work of cinematic art.

YOU KNOW YOU'RE A
DEMOCRAT if...

★ ★ ★

You think the television show
The West Wing is reality TV...
or should be.

YOU KNOW YOU'RE A
REPUBLICAN if...

★ ★ ★

To protest France's undermining
of the U.S., you refuse to drink
any French wine that's over
$50 a bottle.

YOU KNOW YOU'RE A
DEMOCRAT if...

★ ★ ★

You still drink French wines,
but you've sworn off
Terminator movies.

YOU KNOW YOU'RE A
REPUBLICAN if...

★ ★ ★

Your daughter's "coming out"
party gets special mention in the
society page of the paper.

YOU KNOW YOU'RE A
DEMOCRAT if...

★ ★ ★

Your son's "coming out" party
is written up in the
Gay Alliance newsletter.

83

YOU KNOW YOU'RE A
REPUBLICAN if...

★ ★ ★

You feel you must hide your secret passion for reading *Rolling Stone*.

YOU KNOW YOU'RE A
DEMOCRAT if...

★ ★ ★

You feel you must hide your
secret passion for watching
stock car racing.

YOU KNOW YOU'RE A
REPUBLICAN if...

★ ★ ★

You philosophically oppose
government welfare plans, but
you cash your Social Security
checks religiously.

YOU KNOW YOU'RE A
DEMOCRAT if...

★ ★ ★

You're philosophically appalled by corporate America's emphasis on profits, but you're sure happy your pension fund is booming.

YOU KNOW YOU'RE A
REPUBLICAN if...

★ ★ ★

You think Florida election officials
are fair and unbiased.

YOU KNOW YOU'RE A
DEMOCRAT if...

★ ★ ★

You think "fair Florida elections"
is a contradiction in terms.

YOU KNOW YOU'RE A
REPUBLICAN if...

★ ★ ★

You've never seen a government
social services program that you
thought was worth increasing
your taxes for.

YOU KNOW YOU'RE A
DEMOCRAT if...

★ ★ ★

You've never seen a social program
that you weren't willing to spend
other taxpayers' money on.

YOU KNOW YOU'RE A
REPUBLICAN if...

★ ★ ★

In protest you change your middle name from "Jefferson."

YOU KNOW YOU'RE A
DEMOCRAT if...

★ ★ ★

In protest you remove the letter
"W" from your keyboard.

YOU KNOW YOU'RE A
REPUBLICAN if...

★ ★ ★

You prefer your steaks rare and
your jokes raw.

YOU KNOW YOU'RE A
DEMOCRAT if...

★ ★ ★

You prefer your vegetables raw,
you don't eat meat, and you don't
tell jokes...because jokes are about
victimhood and you want to rid
the world of victimhood, and you
don't want to have any part of
it...unless the jokes are about
Republicans.

YOU KNOW YOU'RE A
REPUBLICAN if...

★ ★ ★

Your favorite union is the
Union Pacific Railroad.

YOU KNOW YOU'RE A
DEMOCRAT if...

★ ★ ★

Your favorite union is the Screen
Actors Guild or the AFL-CIO or
maybe the National Education
Association or...oh heck, just
about any union will do.

YOU KNOW YOU'RE A
REPUBLICAN if...

★ ★ ★

You're very proud of your house-keeper's son who is serving in the U.S. military.

YOU KNOW YOU'RE A
DEMOCRAT if...

★ ★ ★

You don't personally know anyone
who is serving in the U.S. military.

YOU KNOW YOU'RE A
REPUBLICAN if...

★ ★ ★

You firmly believe in personal privacy in the bedroom, but you draw the line at same-sex couplings.

YOU KNOW YOU'RE A
DEMOCRAT if...

★ ★ ★

You firmly believe in personal
privacy in the bedroom, but
the thought of two Republicans
procreating sends shivers
down your spine.

YOU KNOW YOU'RE A
REPUBLICAN if...

★ ★ ★

You read about the persons you
admire most in *Fortune*.

YOU KNOW YOU'RE A
DEMOCRAT if...

★ ★ ★

You read about the persons you
admire most in *Variety*.

YOU KNOW YOU'RE A
REPUBLICAN if...

★ ★ ★

Your fondest memories of high
school are your first kiss and
your first DUI.

YOU KNOW YOU'RE A
DEMOCRAT if...

★ ★ ★

Your fondest memories of high school are your first kiss and your first Save the Earth rally.

YOU KNOW YOU'RE A
REPUBLICAN if...

★ ★ ★

Grilled venison was the main
course at your Rotary Club's
banquet honoring you as
"Business Person of the Year."

YOU KNOW YOU'RE A
DEMOCRAT if...

★ ★ ★

Roasted eggplant was the main
course at the Sierra Club chapter
banquet honoring you as
"Non-humanoid Animals
Protector of the Year."

YOU KNOW YOU'RE A
REPUBLICAN if...

★ ★ ★

You still believe the country
would have been better off if
Richard Nixon had defeated
John Kennedy.

YOU KNOW YOU'RE A
DEMOCRAT if...

★ ★ ★

You're still waiting for another
Kennedy—any Kennedy—to
run for president.

YOU KNOW YOU'RE A
REPUBLICAN if...

★ ★ ★

You believe the best way to
increase tax revenues is to cut
taxes, thus stimulating consumer
purchasing, which in turn will
boost business confidence,
investing, and job growth,
eventually yielding higher overall
tax revenues. If that doesn't
work, cut taxes more.

YOU KNOW YOU'RE A
DEMOCRAT if...

★ ★ ★

You believe the best way to
increase tax revenues
is to increase taxes.

YOU KNOW YOU'RE A
REPUBLICAN if...

★ ★ ★

You're totally baffled by the
Israeli–Palestinian conflict, but
you're certain the Democratic
plan is even worse.

YOU KNOW YOU'RE A
DEMOCRAT if...

★ ★ ★

You're totally flummoxed by the
Israeli–Palestinian conflict, but
you think the Republicans have
messed it up.

YOU KNOW YOU'RE A
REPUBLICAN if...

★ ★ ★

Your father warned you about
marrying a gold digging
babe...unless she signs a
prenuptial agreement.

YOU KNOW YOU'RE A
DEMOCRAT if...

★ ★ ★

Your mother warned you against marrying a man who is so focused on his career and making money he has no time for soul-searching conversations.

YOU KNOW YOU'RE A
REPUBLICAN if...

★ ★ ★

You despise huge federal
deficits unless a Republican
president is in office.

YOU KNOW YOU'RE A
DEMOCRAT if...

★ ★ ★

You dislike the huge federal
debt unless your favorite social
programs are threatened.

YOU KNOW YOU'RE A
REPUBLICAN if...

★ ★ ★

Your idea of "grassroots" politics
means lamenting the terrible
burden of taxes while you're
with your golfing buddy on
the 18th green.

YOU KNOW YOU'RE A
DEMOCRAT if...

★ ★ ★

Your idea of "grassroots"
politics means complaining
about the Republican fundraising
advantage while sharing a joint
with your pals.

YOU KNOW YOU'RE A
REPUBLICAN if...

★ ★ ★

Your car displays a bumper sticker
saying, "The Lord giveth and the
Democrats taketh away."

YOU KNOW YOU'RE A
DEMOCRAT if...

★ ★ ★

Your bumper sticker says,
"Don't blame me. I voted for Al."

You own two cows.
Your neighbor has only one.
So?

YOU KNOW YOU'RE A
DEMOCRAT if...

★ ★ ★

You own two cows.
Your neighbor has none.
He doesn't want a cow;
he wants a pig.
You insist the government give
him a cow; pigs are bad for you.
You still have two cows.
You are happy.

YOU KNOW YOU'RE A
REPUBLICAN if...

★ ★ ★

You liked high school.
You studied hard enough to get into
the college you wanted to attend.
You had a girlfriend with nice hair.
Life was good.

YOU KNOW YOU'RE A
DEMOCRAT if...

★ ★ ★

You couldn't wait to get out of high school.

You either were a feminist or dated one.

You studied your brains off.

You joined the debate team or the school paper or, better yet, both.

You wore black.

YOU KNOW YOU'RE A
REPUBLICAN if...

★ ★ ★

You got a "B" on your Western
Civilization midterm paper.
You also got a date with the
girl who sits next to you for
tomorrow's big game.
College is even better than
high school!

YOU KNOW YOU'RE A
DEMOCRAT if...

★ ★ ★

You got a "B" on your Western Civilization midterm paper.
You plan to spend the weekend revising it and on Monday will beg the professor to let you resubmit it.
You'll need to break your date with that big doofus who sits next to you. What were you thinking?

YOU KNOW YOU'RE A
REPUBLICAN if...

★ ★ ★

Your car runs on regular
unleaded gas, but you buy
supreme because you like the
extra kick you think it gives.

YOU KNOW YOU'RE A
DEMOCRAT if...

★ ★ ★

You own a gas-electric hybrid car
with lousy power, but you look
down your nose at everyone who
is passing you on the highway.

YOU KNOW YOU'RE A
REPUBLICAN if...

★ ★ ★

You paid $1,000 to stuff the head
of the trophy buck you shot.
You share the venison with your
business partner.

YOU KNOW YOU'RE A
DEMOCRAT if...

★ ★ ★

You paid $1,000 for a guided trout fishing excursion that was, of course, strictly catch and release.

YOU KNOW YOU'RE A
REPUBLICAN if...

★ ★ ★

You resent paying union dues
because you never like the
politicians the union endorses...
even though you sure like the
union pay scale.

YOU KNOW YOU'RE A
DEMOCRAT if...

★ ★ ★

You always vote for the candidates
your union endorses...as long as
they oppose "right-to-work" laws.

YOU KNOW YOU'RE A
REPUBLICAN if...

★ ★ ★

There are three people in your household and you own four vehicles...not counting the ATVs.

YOU KNOW YOU'RE A
DEMOCRAT if...

★ ★ ★

The three cars you and your wife
drive all get good mileage.

YOU KNOW YOU'RE A
REPUBLICAN if...

★ ★ ★

You have a home aquarium.
The big fish kills the little fish.
So you get another big fish.
They fight constantly. "Animals
are like that," you think.

YOU KNOW YOU'RE A
DEMOCRAT if...

★ ★ ★

You have a home aquarium.
The big fish kills the little fish.
You hold a funeral for the little
fish. You are at a loss for what to
do. You give away the big fish.
You put the empty aquarium in
the attic. "Whew, no more
fighting," you think.

YOU KNOW YOU'RE A
REPUBLICAN if...

★ ★ ★

You bought yourself a
used Ford pickup.
Your friend's dad bought
her a new Mustang.
You are envious.
You want to swap dads.

YOU KNOW YOU'RE A
DEMOCRAT if...

★ ★ ★

Your dad bought you a
cute new Mustang.
You feel guilty.
You feel guilty every day.
You do nothing.

YOU KNOW YOU'RE A
REPUBLICAN if...

★ ★ ★

You think government agencies
should be run like businesses,
with management free to fire
employees at will.

YOU KNOW YOU'RE A
DEMOCRAT if...

★ ★ ★

You think businesses should be
run like government agencies,
with workers free to sue their
employers at will...if someone
tries to fire them.

YOU KNOW YOU'RE A
REPUBLICAN if...

★ ★ ★

You don't pray much yourself,
but you zealously defend the
idea of prayer in school.

YOU KNOW YOU'RE A
DEMOCRAT if...

★ ★ ★

You fight for the separation of church and state with religious zeal, even though you don't pray much yourself.

YOU KNOW YOU'RE A
REPUBLICAN if...

★ ★ ★

You spend considerable amounts
of your own time and money
on causes you're devoted to...
like gun ownership.

YOU KNOW YOU'RE A
DEMOCRAT if...

★ ★ ★

You devote considerable time
to spending taxpayers' money
on causes you support...
like gun control.

YOU KNOW YOU'RE A
REPUBLICAN if...

★ ★ ★

You deplore high taxes but you expect good roads from the city all the way out to your horse farm.

YOU KNOW YOU'RE A
DEMOCRAT if...

★ ★ ★

You think the populace should use mass transit to commute to work, but you deplore the terrible roads out to your house in the woods.

147

YOU KNOW YOU'RE A
REPUBLICAN if...

★ ★ ★

You oppose government subsidized transit, but you expect the public works department to fix that pothole on your street...now!

YOU KNOW YOU'RE A
DEMOCRAT if...

★ ★ ★

You support spending millions on taxpayer-subsidized mass transit used by a tiny fraction of the populace while thousands of fellow taxpayers are stuck in traffic jams on overcrowded highways wasting vast amounts of gas.

YOU KNOW YOU'RE A
REPUBLICAN if...

★ ★ ★

When you were in college you
looked forward to owning your
own business.

YOU KNOW YOU'RE A
DEMOCRAT if...

★ ★ ★

When you were in college you
considered starting a commune
that would make hemp rope.

YOU KNOW YOU'RE A
REPUBLICAN if...

★ ★ ★

You thank God every day for the gifts He has bestowed upon you and your family, especially your tax-free inheritance.

YOU KNOW YOU'RE A
DEMOCRAT if...

★ ★ ★

You thank God every day for the strength She gives you to fight for truth, justice, and punitive damage awards.

YOU KNOW YOU'RE A
REPUBLICAN if...

★ ★ ★

You're dealt great cards, win big playing poker, gloat obnoxiously, but agree to buy the beer at the next game.

YOU KNOW YOU'RE A
DEMOCRAT if...

★ ★ ★

You beat your tennis partner
soundly two games in a row,
feel guilty, call it luck, and suggest
you play three out of five.

YOU KNOW YOU'RE A
REPUBLICAN if...

★ ★ ★

Your dog gets better health care
than your gardener.

YOU KNOW YOU'RE A
DEMOCRAT if...

★ ★ ★

Regardless of the cost, you support free, unlimited, universal health care including coverage for maternity care, hearing aids, bone marrow transplants, prosthetics, orthodontics, dental floss, teeth whitening, Botox injections, earwax cleaning, and, oh yeah, pet care too.

YOU KNOW YOU'RE A
REPUBLICAN if...

★ ★ ★

You thought your college professors
were all flaming liberals.

YOU KNOW YOU'RE A
DEMOCRAT if...

★ ★ ★

You are a college professor.

YOU KNOW YOU'RE A
REPUBLICAN if...

★ ★ ★

Your father made a bundle
as the producer of the
Jerry Springer Show.

YOU KNOW YOU'RE A
DEMOCRAT if...

★ ★ ★

You finally met your real
father as a guest on the
Jerry Springer Show.

YOU KNOW YOU'RE A
REPUBLICAN if...

★ ★ ★

Your wife prefers that you shave
your face every day.

YOU KNOW YOU'RE A
DEMOCRAT if...

★ ★ ★

Your wife prefers *not* to shave her
legs or armpits, but it's okay if
you shave your head.

YOU KNOW YOU'RE A
REPUBLICAN if...

★ ★ ★

You keep up to date from the only
unbiased news source around,
Fox News.

YOU KNOW YOU'RE A
DEMOCRAT if...

★ ★ ★

You keep up to date watching
MTV News.

YOU KNOW YOU'RE A
REPUBLICAN if...

★ ★ ★

You think every Democrat is a
closet Communist.

YOU KNOW YOU'RE A
DEMOCRAT if...

★ ★ ★

You think every Republican is closeted.

YOU KNOW YOU'RE A
REPUBLICAN if...

★ ★ ★

Your idea of "welfare reform" is
handing out pamphlets that say,
"Get a job."

YOU KNOW YOU'RE A
DEMOCRAT if...

★ ★ ★

Your idea of "welfare reform" is
ending corporate tax breaks.

YOU KNOW YOU'RE A
REPUBLICAN if...

★ ★ ★

Your source for illegal drugs is
your maid.

YOU KNOW YOU'RE A
DEMOCRAT if...

★ ★ ★

Your source for illegal drugs is
your uncle.

YOU KNOW YOU'RE A
REPUBLICAN if...

★ ★ ★

Your tennis shoes cost more than
your maid's weekly salary.

YOU KNOW YOU'RE A
DEMOCRAT if...

★ ★ ★

Your tennis shoes cost more than
your car.

YOU KNOW YOU'RE A
REPUBLICAN if...

★ ★ ★

You think the secret to a youthful
appearance is a good personal
trainer and a great plastic surgeon.

174

YOU KNOW YOU'RE A
DEMOCRAT if...

★ ★ ★

You think the secret to a youthful appearance is yoga, soy milk, and a quiet plastic surgeon.

YOU KNOW YOU'RE A
REPUBLICAN if...

★ ★ ★

You think Rush Limbaugh is an intellectual.

YOU KNOW YOU'RE A
DEMOCRAT if...

★ ★ ★

Your think Barbara Streisand is an
insightful political commentator.

YOU KNOW YOU'RE A
REPUBLICAN if...

★ ★ ★

You and your third spouse
vehemently oppose same-sex
marriages.

YOU KNOW YOU'RE A
DEMOCRAT if...

★ ★ ★

You firmly believe marriage should only be between consenting adults of the same species...for now.

YOU KNOW YOU'RE A
REPUBLICAN if...

★ ★ ★

You resent John Kerry for one
thing: He's got nice hair.

YOU KNOW YOU'RE A
DEMOCRAT if...

★ ★ ★

You admire John Kerry for all the ways he reminds you of John Kennedy: He's a Democrat...from Massachusetts...named John...and...and...he's got nice hair.

YOU KNOW YOU'RE A
REPUBLICAN if...

★ ★ ★

You blame your obesity on your
hectic schedule and your
unrestricted expense account.

YOU KNOW YOU'RE A
DEMOCRAT if...

★ ★ ★

You blame your obesity on every
fast-food restaurant you've ever
visited, your neighborhood grocery
store, all the cookie manufacturers,
and your mother...and you're
gonna sue 'em all!

YOU KNOW YOU'RE A
REPUBLICAN if...

★ ★ ★

You support George W. Bush's
plan to put a man on Mars.

YOU KNOW YOU'RE A
DEMOCRAT if...

★ ★ ★

You want that man to *be*
George W. Bush.

YOU KNOW YOU'RE A
REPUBLICAN if...

★ ★ ★

You despise Hollywood celebrities who think their political opinions should be heard...unless they're named Arnold or Charlton.

YOU KNOW YOU'RE A
DEMOCRAT if...

★ ★ ★

You're thrilled when Hollywood celebrities put their star power behind a cause...unless it's running for governor of California.

YOU KNOW YOU'RE A
REPUBLICAN if...

★ ★ ★

You think every American child is entitled to a great high school education, as long as your taxes aren't increased to pay for it.

YOU KNOW YOU'RE A
DEMOCRAT if...

★ ★ ★

You think every American is entitled to a government-paid college education, even if they don't finish high school.

YOU KNOW YOU'RE A
REPUBLICAN if...

★ ★ ★

You plan to become a generous
philanthropist.

YOU KNOW YOU'RE A
DEMOCRAT if...

★ ★ ★

You plan to help out at the local soup kitchen one of these days.

YOU KNOW YOU'RE A
REPUBLICAN if...

★ ★ ★

You want to stem the tide of illegal immigrants getting into the U.S....but then again, somebody's got to mow your lawn.

YOU KNOW YOU'RE A
DEMOCRAT if...

★ ★ ★

You sort of sympathize with undocumented workers ("illegal immigrants" sounds so, well, harsh), but the unions want the borders closed and...oh, shoot, you're just so confused!

YOU KNOW YOU'RE A
REPUBLICAN if...

★ ★ ★

You're thrilled about government financial support of church-based social programs, as long as it's not for Islamic churches.

YOU KNOW YOU'RE A
DEMOCRAT if...

★ ★ ★

You insist upon a strict separation of church and state, unless it threatens your daughter's scholarship to Notre Dame.

195

YOU KNOW YOU'RE A
REPUBLICAN if...

★ ★ ★

Your minister says he will pray for
your soul if you pay for a new gym.

YOU KNOW YOU'RE A
DEMOCRAT if...

★ ★ ★

Your minister says she knows your soul is doing just fine, but could you please bake some cookies to raise money for a new gym.

YOU KNOW YOU'RE A
REPUBLICAN if...

★ ★ ★

Your idea of "compassionate conservatism" means giving your employees praise instead of a raise.

YOU KNOW YOU'RE A
DEMOCRAT if...

★ ★ ★

Your idea of "liberalism" means
using other people's money liberally
for the causes you support.

199

YOU KNOW YOU'RE A
REPUBLICAN if...

★ ★ ★

You visited Disneyland as a kid,
and the Magic Kingdom castle
reminded you of your family's
summer home.

YOU KNOW YOU'RE A
DEMOCRAT if...

★ ★ ★

You visited Disneyland as a kid and thought the depiction of the animatronic bears was insensitive and specieist.

YOU KNOW YOU'RE A
REPUBLICAN if...

★ ★ ★

You blame "affirmative action" for keeping your son from getting into the law school you attended. His grades and test scores weren't so hot, but, by God, he should have been a "legacy!"

YOU KNOW YOU'RE A
DEMOCRAT if...

★ ★ ★

You want law schools to admit minority applicants with lower test scores, although you sure didn't consider race in hiring your own lawyer.

YOU KNOW YOU'RE A
REPUBLICAN if...

★ ★ ★

You didn't understand the cynical
jokes about the Republicans on
the previous pages.

YOU KNOW YOU'RE A
DEMOCRAT if...

★ ★ ★

Your feelings were hurt by some of
the mean jokes about Democrats on
the previous pages.

About the Author

Frank Benjamin is the pseudonym of a university vice president who is (a) cautious, (b) cowardly, (c) modest, (d) all of the above (or perhaps (e) just fond of multiple-choice tests). Now working in the bustling arena of online education, Frank enjoys regular contact with business executives and governors of both political stripes whom, he notes graciously, "usually can laugh at themselves." Usually.